T

A Red Fox Book

Published by Random House Children's Books
20 Vauxhall Bridge Road, London SW1V 2SA

A division of The Random House Group Ltd
London  Melbourne  Sydney  Auckland
Johannesburg and agencies throughout the world

1 3 5 7 9 10 8 6 4 2

Printed and bound in China

THE RANDOM HOUSE GROUP Limited Reg. No. 954009

ISBN 0 09 941116 4

# THE LITTLE BOOK OF

**SUMMER COOL**

HOT TIPS FOR COOL HOLIDAYS!

JOHN BYRNE

RED FOX

*For Kim Morgan*

INTRODUCTION

Yahoo! It's summer at last!
No school, no homework, no
idea what to do? Don't worry,
I've jam packed this cool
collection with lots of tips,
tricks and wheezes to make sure
that rain or shine, home or abroad
you have your best summer ever.
(And as a special extra bonus lots
of these ideas will keep you cool
the rest of the year as well!)
Happy holiday!

Red Fox

# A DATE WITH YOUR DIARY

On the first day of the holidays, write down all your hopes and plans for the summer and then look back at what you wrote on the day before you go back. Although everything may not have gone as you planned, the chances are some nice things happened which you weren't expecting, too. And even if the summer wasn't so good, you can think about what went wrong and see if there are any lessons you can learn to prevent the same mistakes happening next year.

# DIG THIS!

You don't have to be on a desert island to enjoy a good treasure hunt. Get someone to hide the 'treasure' carefully and then hide ten or more clues in the surrounding area. Each clue should lead to the next one and the more riddles and puzzles to be solved the better. Chocs or sweets in gold wrappers will do for the 'treasure'... the fun of a treasure hunt is in the hunting itself.

DID YOU FIND MY TREASURE BY USING A MAP?
NO- YOUR PARROT'S JUST NO GOOD AT KEEPING SECRETS!

# A TASTE FOR ADVENTURE!

If you're lucky enough to travel to a different country for your holiday or even if you're in a different part of the country, try the local food. From yam to sushi to Yorkshire pud, most parts of the world have tasty regional dishes that it would be a real shame to miss. You may not like every dish but at least when you're asked about your holiday menu, you won't have to bite your tongue.

# FOR YOUR OWN A-MUSEUM-MENT!

You may think museums are dusty, fusty old places that you'd most like to avoid on holiday, but these days there are so many different kinds of museum, you almost need a museum to exhibit them all. From aeroplanes to battleships, the cinema to buses and trains, whatever you're into, there may well be a museum full of nothing else.

# JUST TO REMIND YOU...

Whatever else you do this summer, try hard to get in a relaxed holiday frame of mind and put your worries to one side. After all if you are constantly worrying about problems at school or at home, the summer will be gone before you even notice it's around. When you finally turn your mind back to your problems after a stress free summer, you'll be in much better shape to get them sorted out once and for all.

HOW CAN I GET INTO A HOLIDAY MOOD?
ASK TEACHER – HE GETS IN MOODS ALL YEAR ROUND!

# SPEAK UP!

In or out of school, lessons are easier to learn if you make them fun. If you plan to use a foreign language while on holiday, the more chances you give yourself to practise, the better you'll get. So don't just speak the language when you have to, try using it to have fun with, too. From I Spy to Travel Scrabble, playing your favourite games in a new language will help you to learn more words, and to make best use of the words you already know.

# HAND OUT
# A HOLIDAY!

Even if you can't afford to send
someone on an expenses paid trip to
the Bahamas, you can still give them
a well-earned break. For instance if
Mum or Dad usually does the cooking,
you could offer to help out. Older
people might appreciate help with
shopping or errands, while anyone
bringing up young kids will certainly
welcome a helping hand. It's surprising
how doing some good puts you in a
much sunnier frame of mind, too!

# SITTING PRETTY!

You know what it's like on holiday planes and trains - squashed, crowded and not enough seats to go round. Simply cut out the note opposite and hide it in your pocket until you need a bit of extra leg room. Then simply show it to the people near you and say: 'Can anyone read this for me, please? Doctor's handwriting is so difficult'. You'll have the row of seats (if not the entire carriage) to yourself before you can say Atishoo!

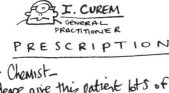

# AVOID
# CAR-TASTROPHES!

If you suffer from car sickness on long journeys, here's an old trick which may make life easier for you. Simply spread a sheet of newspaper on the car seat and sit on it, then put another sheet of newspaper between your feet and the floor of the car. We're not exactly sure why it works, but it seems to, for quite a lot of people. (But if it doesn't, make sure you roll down the window - otherwise the newspaper may come in handy for quite a different purpose!)

# GET MUGGED!

You've heard of beauty contests, but how about holding an ugly contest? Yes, it's true that everyone is beautiful in their own way... but passport photos have a strange way of making everyone look like they come from another planet. Get all you classmates to bring in their worst mugshots on the last day of term and award prizes for things like 'strangest expression' or 'worst hair day'. Teachers can bring their photos in, too - although when it comes to funny faces they're bound to have a head start.

# GOOD TIMING!

Even if you don't go away this year, you can still take a trip - not to another place, to another time. Visit your local library and see if you can find any old photographs or maps of the place where you live, then compare them to the same scenes right now. You'll be surprised how interesting it can be. (And don't forget that in another hundred years' time, someone else may be coming to the library to read all about you!)

LOOK - IN THE OLD DAYS OUR AREA WAS FULL OF WILDLIFE AND FIERCE CREATURES!
YOU'RE GOING TO MEET SOME MORE FIERCE CREATURES IF YOU DON'T STOP SHOUTING!
LIBRARY
QUIET PLEASE!

# HARD TO SWALLOW?

Taking tablets and getting injections may not be much fun - but if you're going somewhere where malaria or tropical bugs are a danger, the consequences of not doing this stuff could be a lot worse. Vaccinations are nothing to be scared of - the small pinpricks only last a few seconds. And if you take your tablets at a regular time (such as breakfast) every day, you can soon stop thinking about them and get on to the serious business of having healthy holiday fun.

# MANY HAPPY RETURNS!

If you're lucky enough to holiday abroad you'll enjoy discovering all the sights, sounds and tastes of a new country... but remember to give as well as take. The local people answering your questions may have their own questions to ask you and if they're helping you learn the language, they might like the chance to practise their English, too.

# HAVE THE LAST LAUGH!

Sometimes it just happens. The holiday you've been looking forward to all year goes from bad to worse, from the horrible hotel you're stuck in for two weeks to the rotten rain clouds that drench you from start to finish. Disappointment is always hard to cope with, but it's usually the things that go wrong that make the funniest holiday memories later on. You will laugh about all this some day... so why not save time and start laughing right now?

I'D LIKE TO COMPLAIN — MY HOLIDAY WENT PERFECTLY SO THERE WAS NOTHING TO HAVE A GOOD LAUGH ABOUT!
TRAVEL AGENT

# SOUND ADVICE

If the rows on family car journeys about what music to play get so loud that you can't hear any music in the first place, why not make up a compilation tape? Mixing a dash of Dad's classical music with your sister's boybands and your older brother's heavy metal will mean that everyone gets to listen to what they want to some of the time... and the rest of the time you might be surprised to find yourself enjoying music you don't normally listen to.

# CHANGE DIRECTION!

If you need to ask directions while on holiday do remember that some people often give wrong directions simply because they don't want to say, 'I don't know'. (Bet you've done it once or twice, too!) So if you really don't want to get lost, ask at least two people. If the answers are different, keep asking people until you get directions that a couple of people agree on (by which time you may well have reached your destination all by yourself!).

# BEAT THE BODYBUILDERS!

Whether you're male or female, musclebound mugs flashing their pecs around the beach can quickly get on your nerves. Well here's a way you can outshine them all. Simply put your fingertips together in front of your chest and challenge the strongest person on the beach to hold your arms just above the elbows and pull them apart they'll fail no matter how strong they are. Then you can get back to enjoying the sun, while they bury their head in the sand.

GRUNT!
THEY CAN PULL AS MUCH AS THEY LIKE – YOU'LL STILL BE ABLE TO PULL THIS TRICK OFF!
GROAN!
MUM

# FUN FACTORY

If you don't enjoy plodding around museums and art galleries, would you prefer a trip to a sweet factory, a recording studio or a look at computer games being put together? Many businesses arrange tours and if there's somewhere you'd like to visit which doesn't you could try contacting their Public Relations department. You'll have a better chance of success if you can organise a group visit and with the chance of some free samples at the end of the tour, you should have lots of volunteers.

# SLOW, SLOW, QUICK, QUICK, SLOW

Even though your brain knows it's on holiday, your body may take longer to catch on. With lessons, chores and homework to squeeze in during term time, we can get used to rushing around, and that rush rush attitude can continue into holiday time, so that we end up back at school before we know it. Take some time at the start of the summer to relax and slow down to a holiday pace – the fun of summer will last longer and your energy for enjoying it will last a lot longer, too!

# CROC 'N' ROLL

Summer may be the time for running about... but if you never win races, you may soon find yourself running out of steam. Here's a team race game that gives everyone an equal chance. The teams line up with players one behind the other, then they have to crouch down low and race for the finish line in this position. This fast, fun game is called a 'crocodile race', either because both teams look like crocodiles, or because playing it could lead to some hilarious snaps.

IN A CROCODILE RACE ALL PLAYERS HAVE TO STAY CROUCHED DOWN AND KEEP HOLDING ON TO EACH OTHER!
NOW THAT'S WHAT I CALL THE FULL LOWDOWN!

# SITTING PRETTY!

If your family has booked seats on a
train or plane it's a good idea to work
out in advance where you want to sit,
before the usual squabbling starts.
The window seat is the one to go for
if you want to enjoy the view, while the
seat next to the aisle is best if you
want to get up often without tripping
over everyone else's legs. Whichever
you choose, avoid the middle seat
- you'll end up with no view, no room
to move and usually no place to rest
your arms either.

# WRITE ON!

Stuck for something to read over the holidays? Why not choose a book by the author who knows what you enjoy best... YOU! To write a book, all you need is a pen and paper and your own imagination. You can write what you like because no one has to see it except you and, whatever you like to read, you'll be surprised how much fun making up your own stories can be.

# SNAP HAPPY!

If you're a keen photographer, holiday time is the ideal time to get great pictures. And if you haven't taken photos before maybe you should think about joining your school camera club to get some practise. But as you're snapping away, do remember to get in the occasional photo yourself. It's amazing how many people come back from holiday with lots of photos of the family having fun... and no record that they were there at all!

LOOK! IT'S A PHOTO OF TEACHER AND A SNAKE ON OUR SCHOOL TRIP!
WHERE'S TEACHER?
INSIDE THE SNAKE.

# SAFARI, SO GOOD

This summer why not find out about some really fascinating creatures - your family! Yes, we know you probably see them every day, but it's because we're together most of the time that families often take each other for granted. Why not see if you can discover something new about each one of your family? A like, a dislike, a story from when they were younger - whatever you learn you're bound to find that your family is a lot more interesting then you think.

# QUICK ON THE DRAW!

No matter how good you are at foreign languages, there's bound to be a time when you're lost for words, and that's when pictures come in handy. If you can't make what you are saying understood, try drawing the thing you want to buy, find or do. Even when this trick doesn't work, it makes people smile and smiling is a good way to make friends no matter what language you speak.

# A-TENT-TION PLEASE!

Going camping for the first time can be a lot of fun, but it can also be a wash out if you're struggling to put up the tent in the pouring rain. So if you or your family have bought a nice new tent, make sure you have a 'trial run' at putting it up somewhere before. That way you'll work out how to do it properly (and if all the bits are there) before you venture out into the wild.

IT SAYS IN THE MANUAL WE SHOULD HOLD OUR TENT UP WITH PEGS
PEG MAY BE YOUR SISTER, BUT I DON'T THINK SHE'S GOING TO STAY THERE ALL NIGHT!

# GIVE US A BREAK!

If you've had a great holiday, or if you're due to go somewhere exciting, it's natural to want to share your excitement with the whole school. But do remember that not everybody is lucky enough to be able to go on holiday, and for some people homelife may be no picnic either. By all means chat to your schoolmates about your terrific two weeks, but remember you've got to live with them the other fifty weeks of the year, so it's a good idea to let them get a word in, too.

# SUMMER SAVER

Postcards, souvenirs, presents and all those holiday treats. It's very easy to run out of holiday money almost before your holiday has even started. If you allow yourself a certain amount of holiday money to spend each day, you'll find your cash lasts a lot longer. You may have to wait to buy something expensive, but that will give you all the more time to decide if it really is special enough to blow your money on in the first place.

# GET THE NEEDLE!

If you get trapped in some dense dangerous jungle (or lost in the local garden centre) here's a handy compass you can make using just a needle and a glass of water. Magnetise the needle by rubbing it with a magnet (a fridge magnet will do fine) and then float it carefully on top of the water, as shown. No matter what way you place it, the needle will slowly move round to point North.

FLOATING A NEEDLE ON TOP OF A GLASS SHOWS US WHAT DIRECTION NORTH IS...
IF YOU DRANK A GLASS OF WATER THAT BIG YOU'D NEED TO KNOW WHAT DIRECTION THE LOO IS, AND FAST!
(NOT ACTUAL SIZE)

# MAIL MERGE

Summer is the ideal time to get into stamp or coin collecting, or to build your collection if these are hobbies you already enjoy. Whether you're abroad and meeting the locals or at home and chatting to tourists, it's a great opportunity to swap coins or to swap addresses and receive some mail with foreign stamps. Do reply to your mail, though - the stamps you see every day are exciting to a collector on the other side of the world.

# DO THE RIGHT LEFT RIGHT THING

You should be careful crossing the road all year round, but do be doubly careful if you're spending the summer on the Continent - looking left and right is fine, but you need to remember that the cars will be coming from the opposite direction to the one you're used to!

# OUTFOXED!

Here's a foxy puzzle for long journeys. Copy the fox shape opposite onto some cardboard, thread some string through the hole and tie a large button to each end. Now challenge your family to remove the string without tearing the fox or untying or breaking the string. They won't be able to. When they give up simply fold the fox in two, and push the strip between the two slits (A) through the hole - it will form a loop on the other side which the buttons can go through!

# HEAR, HEAR

If you always mean to read books during the summer, but find yourself heading back to school with the same unopened pile you started with, try slipping a talking book into your personal stereo every once in a while. That way you can get lost in the pages of a great story without losing out on the rest of your summer activities.

# JUST THE JOB

Now that you're on holiday, why not try a little work? Your parents' work that is. If Mum or Dad work in an office or a factory ask if you can come with them one day. It could make for a very interesting day out (even if they don't work in a sweet factory) and your parents will probably be as proud to show you off as you are of them. You'll certainly get to see your parents in a whole new light... and may even realise why they need a holiday even more than you do.

# FRUITY FEAT

You'll have a healthier holiday if you watch what you eat... and here's a healthy stunt to try. Ask a friend to name two vegetables and one fruit, write them on a strip of paper and tear as shown. Then ask them to mix the names up while you are blindfolded. Even though you can't see you can tell what piece is a fruit or vegetable just by feeling it! The secret? If you write the fruit in the middle of the strip the 'fruit' will have two jagged edges whereas the vegetables will only have one.

PEA APPLE BEAN
PEA
APPLE
BEAN
TEAR HERE
YOUR FRIENDS WILL BE AMAZED UNLESS YOU TELL THEM THE FRUIT, THE WHOLE FRUIT AND NOTHING BUT THE FRUIT!

# FLOWER POWER!

Even humble plants have interesting stories behind them. For instance, we get the name Dandelion from the French *dente de leon* because its spiky leaves look like lion's teeth. You can tell if a friend likes butter by holding a buttercup under their chin and seeing if there's a yellow reflection. And it's said that the Scottish thistle was put in castle moats instead of water to give would-be attackers a short sharp shock. Check the stories behind your local flowers and see how your interest in nature blossoms.

# STAY AHEAD OF THE GAME!

There's one thing that will defeat even the most fearsome computer games warrior... and that's lack of electricity. If you're bringing your games (or any other electrical devices) abroad, don't forget that other countries may not have the same electrical system as ours... or even the same shaped sockets. A universal adapter works in most countries, but it's also a good idea to turn off your games once in a while and enjoy a holiday in the real world.

# IT'S IN THE BAG!

There's nothing as frustrating as forgetting your ball when you're in the mood for a holiday game. Never mind - here's how to make an imaginary one. All you need is a brown paper bag, which you fold over on top to make a 'lip' and then hold it as shown in the picture. Now throw your imaginary ball in the air and as you move the bag under it, snap your fingers at the lip. It really does look and sound like a ball has landed in the bag

# HAVE WE GOT
# SNOOZE FOR YOU

When you're travelling, one of the most
useful things you can bring is a small
pillow. You can prop it against the
window or the side of your seat for a
good snooze, or if it's a really long
journey you may find it a relief to have
some extra padding under your bum.
If you don't fancy having to carry the
pillow around, just bring a pillowcase,
which can be stuffed with socks or
other clothes. Make sure you use
clean socks, though, or your snooze
could turn into a nightmare!

# MEET WITH SUCCESS!

It's fun to do things with people on holiday, but it's also fun to do your own thing. If you're exploring a new country and you want to split up for a while remember to arrange a good place to meet back at. 'Let's meet back here' is fine, if you're somewhere you can easily find your way back to, but it's a good idea to locate a proper landmark and use that as your meeting place. That way even if you do get lost it shouldn't be too hard to ask for directions.

 # THAT'S THE SPIRIT!

Fancy spending the summer in a haunted house? Well, you can make your house appear haunted with this sneaky spirit writing trick. Simply breathe on a handy mirror and a ghostly message will magically appear! EEK! How's it done? If you write the message with your finger beforehand, it will remain invisible until you breathe on the glass.

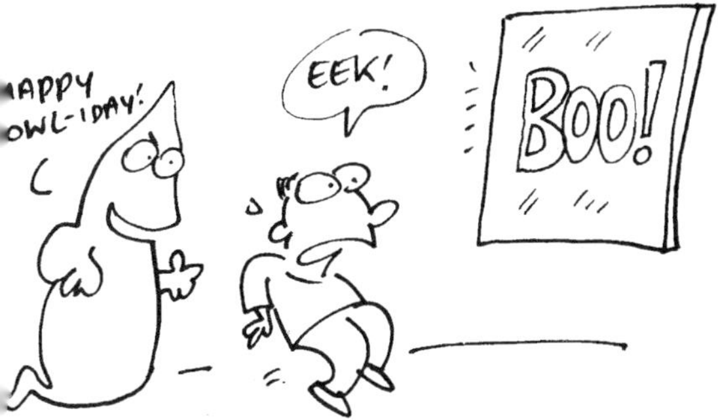
APPY
OWL-IDAY!
EEK!
BOO!

# BRIGHT IDEA

One of the best things about summer is the sunshine. But it can't be said too often that too much sun can do you more harm than good. So always put on suntan lotion before going out and remember that even if your sunglasses look cool, it's worth checking that they really do keep sunrays out before you look at the sun. In fact staring at the sun at all isn't a very bright idea. Why not play safe and set a shining example to everyone else?

# GET SWITCHED ON...
## SWITCH OFF!

For some people going abroad for a holiday is not much fun because they miss TV! So why not start training for your TV-free time right now? You can give yourself a reward when you can manage a whole week away... and don't worry, you'll find the storylines of all your favourite soaps are easy to catch up on. Mind you, when you've realised how many other interesting things there are to do, you may not care any more.

# COMPLETELY BAL-LOONY!

A message in a bottle has been a very exciting and mysterious part of many holiday adventure stories - but chucking bottles or any other junk into the sea is bad for the environment. A better way of sending a message is to tie a note to a balloon (one filled with helium gas is best) and then let the balloon go. Put your address on the note and with any luck you may get a reply. You may have lost a balloon but it's a small price to pay for a new pen pal.

DON'T PUT TOO MUCH AIR IN THE BALLOON OR YOU'LL BE ABLE TO DELIVER YOUR MESSAGE IN PERSON!

# HIT THE RIGHT NOTE!

Holiday time is a great opportunity
to do some of the things you've been
meaning to do, but never got round to.
Maybe there's a hobby you haven't had
time to keep up, a book you've wanted
to read (or would like to re-read) or
a friend you haven't seen for a while.
Making a holiday 'things to do' list will
give you lots to look forward to and
also a great sense of achievement
as you tick things off.

# STRETCH YOURSELF

It may seem daft to be 'warming up' during a hot summer, but proper warming up - stretching your legs and arms, making sure your muscles are ready for action - is something you should always do before playing any summer sports or games. It's important to cool down afterwards as well... that way you'll get the full benefit of summer activities and be fit for action all winter, too.

# A HANDY PASTIME

Here's a game that you can play anywhere and in any language. Paper, Scissors, Rock simply involves two players hiding their hand behind their back and then on the count of three making one of the shapes shown. If Paper and Rock come up, Paper wins (paper can cover rock) Scissors beat Paper (scissors cut paper), and Rock beats Scissors (rock blunts scissors). Two shapes the same is a draw. Seems simple? Try it - you'll be surprised just how much fun you have on your hands!

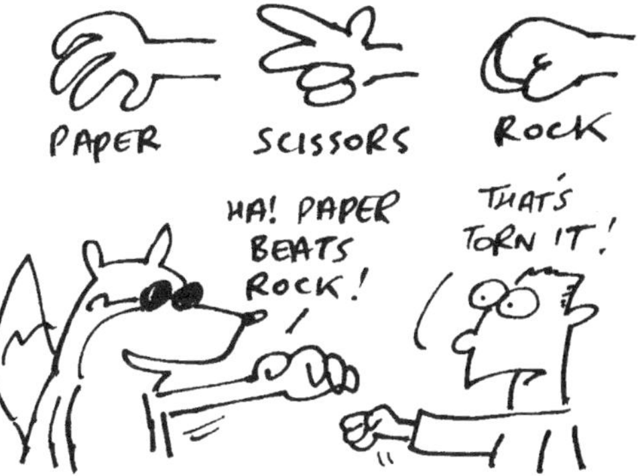
PAPER
SCISSORS
ROCK
HA! PAPER BEATS ROCK!
THAT'S TORN IT!

# CARD TRICK

Just because you're staying at home for the holidays doesn't mean you can't send postcards - simply take a photo of your own house and glue copies of it onto blank cards. Then send the cards through the post. You can be sure that out of all the cards your friends and family receive from strange and exotic places, yours will be the one they never forget!

# MIX 'N' MATCH

You've got the whole summer ahead of you and you'll want to enjoy it to the full, so make sure you organise yourself so that you get the most out of every activity. If you're the energetic type, try to have a few relaxing times between the more hectic days so you'll have your full strength when you need it. On the other hand if you prefer to relax, do try to shake a leg and get out and about every so often - then you'll enjoy the quiet times even more.

# COOL CASH!

Here's a cool coin trick that will work with whatever currency you use. All you need are two coins - it doesn't matter what value so long as one is bigger then the other. Cut a hole in a small piece of paper or card the same size as the smaller coin and challenge someone to pass the bigger coin through the hole without tearing the paper. They won't be able to do it - but you will if you use the sneaky trick opposite. It's a 'hole' new approach.

LARGE COIN

SMALL HOLE

SIMPLY BEND THE PIECE OF PAPER A BIT AND THE LARGER COIN FITS THROUGH!

# MAY THE SAUCE
# BE WITH YOU!

If you or someone in your family is really fussy about food, it is a good idea to take a small bottle of your favourite sauce on holiday. It's fun to try out new food, but the occasional dollop of your favourite taste from home may be enough to help you get to grips with unfamiliar grub and stop you going hungry. Do screw the cap on tightly before you pack it, though - a suitcase full of sauce stains would be in very bad taste!

# PHONEY BUSINESS!

Here's another fearsome feat of
strength to make sure no one kicks
sand in your face on the beach! Simply
flex your powerful muscles and tell the
assembled masses that you are about
to tear a telephone directory in half.
Then take a phone book (an old one)
and tear the first page in half, then
the second, then the third... well you
didn't say you were going to do it
all at once, did you?

 STICKY SITUATION

If you've got a snazzy new suitcase or backpack, you'll want to keep it in good condition. But if you're planning to carry it in the luggage section of a plane, boat or train, you may need to personalise it just a bit. Sticking a Sellotape version of your first initial on the side is a good way to spot your own bag without marking it for good. After you've got your luggage back you can rip the tape off... it's the best way to avoid getting ripped off!

MY LITTLE BROTHER IS REALLY WORRIED ABOUT PEOPLE NICKING HIS BAG...
CHECK IN

# ON COURSE FOR A FUN SUMMER

You spend the whole year learning things at school, so learning things in the summer holidays might not seem like much of a break. The difference is that you can learn things that are fun! Whether it's skateboarding or karate, the saxophone or stilt-walking, there are probably lots of interesting summer courses going on somewhere near you, and putting some time into learning a new skill now can give you hours of fun all year round.

# HOT DOG!

If you're going somewhere exotic for your holidays, you may be worried about snakes, scorpions and other nasty beasties. But home or abroad it's worth remembering that animals don't have to look scary to be dangerous. In particular, be careful of stray dogs - it doesn't take much to startle them and leave you nursing a nasty nip. If you are bitten by an animal, make sure you have it checked by a doctor. Ignoring it and spending the rest of the hols with a nasty bug really would be beastly.

# TAKE YOUR TIME

If you're travelling on a really long plane journey you may get what we call 'jet lag'. It happens when we travel to a country that's in different time zone, but our body clock (the part of our brain that tells us when to get up and go to sleep) still thinks we're at home. Except for making you feel like sleeping even when it's midday, jet lag isn't serious and one good night's sleep usually sorts it out.

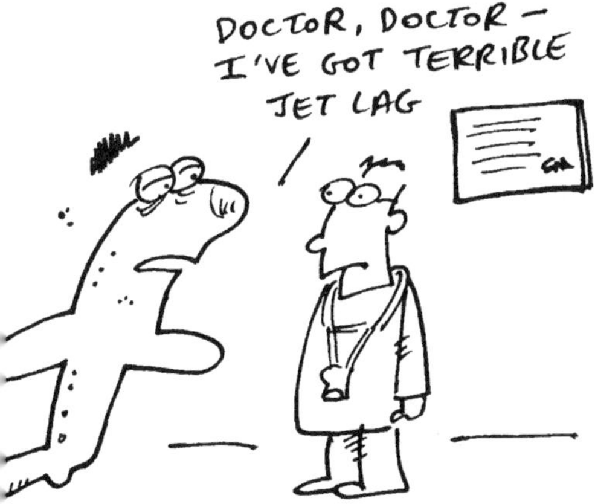
DOCTOR, DOCTOR – I'VE GOT TERRIBLE JET LAG

# DRESS FOR SUCCESS!

Everybody wants to look good in summer - but eating too little to lose weight is very uncool. Choosing your clothes carefully can work wonders. For instance, clothes with thin vertical lines make you look thinner, while clothes with horizontal lines can make you look bigger. But whatever clothes you wear, if you accept yourself as you are you'll be surprised how many other people will think you're pretty cool, too.

# BAG OF TRICKS

Here's a fruity summer puzzle that works with everything from apples to papayas. Show your family or friends nine fruits and four paper bags and ask them to put fruit in each of the bags so that at the end each bag has an odd number of fruits inside. It can't be done, unless you know the secret. Simply put three fruits each into three of the bags and then put the three bags inside the fourth bag.

# EYE SAY,
# EYE SAY, EYE SAY...

On holiday and missing good old British food? Your troubles are over! Simply copy our handy picture onto the inside of your sunglasses and every meal you look at will be magically transformed into a plate of fish 'n' chips. Don't wear the glasses while crossing the road, though, or the only fish you'll see are starfish!

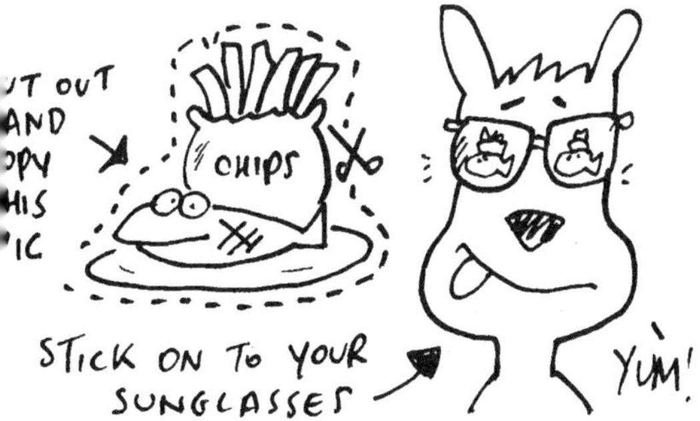
OUT
AND
CHIPS
STICK ON TO YOUR
SUNGLASSES
YUM!

# FOREIGN FEUDS!

Although the scenery may change when you're on holiday, the people in your family don't and squabbles that happen at home are just as likely to take place when you've travelled somewhere else. In fact, sometimes being away from home makes little rows seem far worse. Luckily, the same solutions to family rows work wherever you are - talk through your difficulties and decide together on a solution, it may just give you a holiday free from hassle for good!

# HOT PEPPER!

Eating out in a posh restaurant is a great holiday treat - but if you only get to go to the local greasy cafe, here's a way to add some magic to your meal. Take the salt and pepper shakers and pour out a small mound of both on the table. Now announce that you can separate the salt from the pepper without touching either. Impossible? If you take a comb from your pocket and run it through your hair to build up static, you'll find the comb picks up the pepper, but not the salt. Isn't that electrifying?

# RIDDLE
## OF THE SANDS

If you've got a pair of old shorts, shoes and socks here's a great visual gag for the beach. Stuff the shorts with old newspaper and then put the socks and shoes on the end (also full of paper). Now bury your creation upside down in the sand. When passers-by give you funny looks, say: 'Dad said it was fine to bury him as long as it was just up to his ankles!' Do let people know you're joking as soon as possible or you may get real digging practice - trying to tunnel your way out of prison.

FILL THE MODEL WITH OLD NEWSPAPER
WOW! WHEN YOU BURY IT, IT REALLY LOOKS LIKE SOMEONE'S IN THE SAND!
I AM IN THE SAND! I DUG TOO DEEP WHEN I WAS BURYING!

# IS YOUR HOME
# IN A STATE?

If you don't have a stately home
nearby why not put together a guided
tour of your own house? From Dad's old
football boots (last worn in 1982) to
the crayon marks your baby brother
made on the sitting room wall, every
inch of your house has its own history
and though you may not be able to
charge the public money for seeing it,
your family should get a good laugh
out of a trip down memory lane.

# TAKE A RAINCHECK

You know how it is - just when you have the perfect summer's day out planned, the heavens open and it's a complete washout. At least it is if you haven't made a Rainy Day Box. It's simple - pick some books or comics you'd really like to read or re-read and some CDs or tapes you like listening to and pack them away for a rainy day. You could put some of your favourite sweets in there, too. Then, when rain threatens to spoil your fun, you can dip into your box and save the day.

# SIGN HERE

If you're on holiday overseas don't forget that simple signs and gestures can be very different from the ones you're used to. For instance, in this country we ask for a lift by sticking our thumbs out, while in some other countries the way to do it is to move your hand up and down. See how many differences you can spot on your own holiday (but remember that whatever gesture you use, thumbing a lift on you own is a highly dangerous thing to do no matter where you are).

# MAKE SENSE

New tastes, new sounds, new smells –
there can be lots to take in on holiday.
So why not train yourself to use your
senses properly? Pick a different sense
each day and really concentrate on
getting your information that way. For
instance if you pick 'hearing', listen
hard to the different accents and day
to day noises you hear. Or you might
pick 'smell' and check out the scents
of foreign food, flowers and plants.

# TUMMY TROUBLES

No matter how careful you are, travel enough times and sooner or later you'll probably get a touch of holiday tummy. In most cases it only lasts a day or two, and although it's not much fun, you should be able to stick to your holiday plans if you rest a little, drink lots of water and eat light, non-spicy food. If the problem lasts longer than a few days, it's time to visit the doctor. Don't forget to bring this book with you - there's bound to be a queue in the waiting room!

OH NO! LOOKS LIKE SOMETHING DAD ATE DIDN'T AGREE WITH HIM!
URGH! I FEEL TERRIBLE!
SPEAK FOR YOURSELF... I FEEL GREAT!

# GIVE THIS SOME THOUGHT...

If you want to bring back holiday gifts for your friends (or even souvenirs for yourself) you don't have to go to expensive 'tourist' shops. An unusual seashell, a local magazine... for real friends the most important thing about a holiday gift is that it was chosen specially for them rather than that it cost a lot of money.

So before you open your purse or wallet, put on your thinking cap. Then you can pick a unique gift that could only have come from you.

# MONEY MAKES THE WORLD GO ROUND

Shake out your pockets after a foreign trip and you're sure to find some small coins. If you're not a coin collector, the best thing to do is to pop them into the box you'll find in the arrivals section of most airports. When the box is full, all the different coins are turned into home currency and given to charity. Knowing you're helping a good cause should give you a lift, even when you're on the ground.

# PROMISES, PROMISES!

'Do come and visit us whenever you're in our town!' 'I'll send you a copy of these photos.' On holiday, promises like these are made all they time. Often the promises get broken... and sometimes you wish you'd never made them when the 'friend' you met abroad insists on coming to stay the next year. So make sure you don't make holiday promises you don't intend to (or can't) keep. You'll be glad later on... we promise!

REMEMBER WE MET ON YOUR SAFARI HOLIDAY LAST YEAR? I THOUGHT I'D POP BY FOR A FEW WEEKS...

# ONE BAD APPLE

Have you ever got annoyed when a tourist with a backpack blocked your way in the street? The same thing can happen when you're the tourist. It's also true that all over the world you'll find a small number of people who just aren't very nice. If you run into such a person on holiday remember that it IS just one person. Don't decide that everyone else from that place is horrible, too, and certainly don't let it ruin your holiday.

# THE POST WITH THE MOST!

Sometimes it's difficult to find the right postcards, no matter how hard you try. So why not design your own? If you've brought some blank cards from home, you can try drawing your own impression of the place you're staying, or stick down a bus ticket or some local leaves or plants to really give a sense of the place. (Just don't use your return ticket or you could be staying on holiday for longer than you intended!)

# ANIMAL HOSPITALITY

It's always sad to leave your pet behind when you go on holiday, but it's easier when you know your furry friend has somewhere nice to stay. If you're asking a friend or neighbour to look after the animal, make sure they know what they're getting into. And while you're away, don't forget to put them on top of your holiday present list, so they'll be happy to do the same job again next year.

THANKS FOR LOOKING AFTER MY PET ELEPHANT MR JONES- HOPE YOU'LL DO IT AGAIN NEXT YEAR!

# USE YOUR HEAD

Passports, maps, the address of your hotel - they can all get lost when you're on holiday. So try to keep a few important details in your head. For instance try to memorise the emergency telephone number and the international dialling code that you have to add to your own telephone number before you can call home. Also note the number that contacts an operator if you need to reverse the charges. Whatever the call costs, letting your family know you're safe will make it money well spent.

# PICK UP ON THIS

However many bags you take on summer trips, there's one bag you should not go without - a bag to bring your rubbish back home with you. If you enjoy visiting somewhere you'll want to come back and still find the place at its best. One or two pieces of litter chucked away may not seem very serious, but what if the next visitors decide to do the same? And the next and the next? Caring about the environment is cool all year round - in fact, any other attitude is rubbish!

# ON YOUR BIKE!

Cycling is a fun, healthy holiday activity and even more fun if you try this stunt. Next time you're changing the wheel of your bike, challenge your friends to balance the wheel on one finger, as shown. It's very hard, however strong they are. But no matter how wimpy you might be, if you hold the wheel with two hands first and spin it, you'll find you can transfer it to one finger 'wheely' easily.

START SPINNING THE WHEEL LIKE THIS...
...AND YOU'LL SOON 'GET ROUND' TO USING ONE FINGER!

# CAR-A-OKE

There's nothing like a good old singsong to while away a long car journey - but after a while old favourites like 'Row, Row, Row Your Boat' or 'The Wheels on The Bus' may start to lose their appeal. So why not try the 'karaoke' section of your local record shop. You'll find backing tracks for lots of top pop songs, and even ones your mum and dad will remember. Some of the tapes even come with lyric sheets to read, but don't give one to the driver or you really will have a smash hit.

# HAPPIER NEW YEAR

Try to remember what happened on last year's holiday - what you ate for breakfast, what you did in the afternoon. You'll be surprised at how many small details you've forgotten, which is interesting since it's the niggly details which are likely to cause most of the quarrels on this year's holiday. Since you'll have forgotten them next year, are they really worth fighting about now? Of course not - so forget them and get on with having a real summer to remember!

# WRITE, NOW!

If you're sending postcards to all your
best pals, don't forget to send one
to your best friend of all - yourself.
Wait until the last day of the holidays
and jot down all the best things that
happened and your happiest memories.
When you've been home a few days the
card will arrive and allow you to enjoy
the good feelings your holiday brought
for just that little bit longer.

# 'WASH' YOUR STEP

Wash your hands before meals. Rinse fruit before you eat it. And do check that food hasn't gone off before you tuck in. Yes we know you get this advice at home all year round... but it's doubly important to remember when you're travelling abroad. There are often lots of extra nasty tummy bugs about overseas - and you don't want to give them the chance to sneak up on you. If you do catch something, a couple of days in bed usually sorts things out - but who wants to spend their holidays like that?

# BE A 'GLASS' ACT!

At home or abroad it's a lot healthier to cool down with a bottle of mineral water instead of lots of sugary drinks. And if you can find one of the old-fashioned bottles with a narrow neck you can outwit your friends, too.

Cut a narrow strip of paper and balance it on the bottleneck, as shown, with some coins on top. Can your friends remove the paper without touching the coins or the bottle? It's impossible, no matter how gently they try. But you can, if you know the trick.

SIMPLY TEAR A PIECE OFF THE PAPER ON ONE SIDE, THEN GIVE A SHARP TUG ON THE OTHER!
POP

# MAKE IT SNAPPY!

If you're hoping to meet new people on your holiday, or even if you're sitting next to someone on a long journey and you're shy about starting conversation, try bringing a couple of family photos with you. Almost everybody enjoys talking (or moaning) about their family. And the great thing about photos is that they are interesting even if you don't speak the same language. In fact, before you know it, you may well be asking someone to take a photograph of you and your new-found friend.